# HEALTHY SA
# COOKBOOK

## *THE TOP 50 MOST HEALTHY AND DELICIOUS SALAD RECIPES*

By

*ANITA HANSON*

Copyright © 2015

# Free Bonus

As a small symbol of thanks for buying this book,

I'd like to give a free bonus exclusive to my readers.

This Bonus is called **10 HEALTHY SMOOTHIE RECIPES**

## What The Bonus Include?

- Recipe 1 - Mango Smoothie Surprise
- Recipe 2 - Blueberry Smoothie
- Recipe 3 - Peanut Butter and Banana
- Recipe 4 - Vanilla Yogurt and Blueberry
- Recipe 5 - Chocolate Raspberry
- Recipe 6 - Peach Smoothie
- Recipe 7 - Lemon-Orange Citrus
- Recipe 8 - Apple Smoothie
- Recipe 9 - Pineapple Smoothie
- Recipe 10 - Strawberry Smoothie

## Download The Bonus From Here

http://www.elifemastery.com/10-healthy-smoothie-recipes/

# Table of Contents

# Time To Make 0-15 Minutes

## Recipe 1 - Craisin Salad

### Total Time: 15 Minutes

- **Preparation: 10 Mins**
- **Cooking: 5 Mins**

## *INGREDIENTS*

1 head romaine lettuce, torn into medium sized pieces

2 whole green onions, chopped

1 cup craisins

1⁄4 cup sliced almonds

1⁄2 cup diced celery

1 medium chopped avocado (I have never added this item.) (optional)


### Dressing

1⁄4 cup vegetable oil

2 tbsps cider vinegar

2 tbsps granulated sugar

1⁄2 tsp salt

1⁄4 tsp black pepper or 1⁄4 tsp white pepper

## DIRECTIONS

1. Heat dressing ingredients till sugar dissolves, stir continuously.
2. Cool dressing.
3. Blend salad ingredients.
4. Prior to serving put dressing over salad as well as toss properly.

# Recipe 2 - Cucumber-Zucchini Salad

## Total Time: 5 Minutes

- **Preparation: 5 Mins**
- **Cooking: 0 Mins**

## *INGREDIENTS*

cucumbers, thinly sliced

2 zucchini, thinly sliced

1 small sweet onion, thinly sliced (optional)

1/3 cup vinegar

1/4 cup sugar

1/2 tbsp salt

1 tsp coarse black pepper, fresh cracked

1 pinch red pepper flakes

## DIRECTIONS

1. Set up in alternate layers zucchini, cucumber and onions.
2. Blend WHITE VINEGAR and SUGARS dissolved in 1/2 cup WARM WATER add pepper, salt and smashed red pepper.
3. Include one or two ice cubes to chill.
4. Drain any kind of water created by cucumbers prior to adding the dressing.
5. Permit vegetables to be able to marinate in the dressing a minimum of An hour just before serving.

# Recipe 3 - Apple Carrot Pineapple Salad

## Total Time: 5 Minutes

- **Preparation: 5 Mins**
- **Cooking: 0 Mins**

## *INGREDIENTS*

1 apple, shredded

1 carrot, grated

1⁄2 cup pineapple chunk

2 tbsps plain yogurt

1 dash cinnamon

## <u>DIRECTIONS</u>

1.  Mix all ingredients and serve..

# Recipe 4 - Island Black Bean Salad

## Total Time: 0 Minutes

- **Preparation: 0 Mins**
- **Cooking: 0 Mins**

## *INGREDIENTS*

6 cups cooked black beans

3 cups cooked corn

1/4 cup chopped cilantro

1 chopped red bell pepper

8 scallions, chopped

1 cup Italian dressing

2 tsps cumin

1/2 tbsp black pepper

1 tbsp salt

2 tsps dried oregano

2 limes, juiced

# DIRECTIONS

1. Combine all ingredients in big bowl.
2. Allow it to rest for a couple of hours under refrigeration prior to serving.

# Recipe 5 - Moroccan Carrot Salad

## Total Time: 10 Minutes

- **Preparation: 10 Mins**
- **Cooking: 0 Mins**

## *INGREDIENTS*

6 carrots, grated

1 dash olive oil, to coat the carrots

1 tsp cumin

1 tbsp sugar

chopped fresh parsley

1 dash lemon juice

## <u>DIRECTIONS</u>

1. Grate carrots.
2. Drizzle carrots along with olive oil to coat.
3. Spread using cumin ,toss and sugar .
4. Include sliced fresh parsley as well as a sprinkle of juice of lemons prior to you serve.

# Recipe 6 - Ethiopian Fruit Salad

## Total Time: 10 Minutes

- **Preparation: 10 Mins**
- **Cooking: 0 Mins**

## *INGREDIENTS*

1 ripe mango, peeled and cut in pieces

1 small ripe papaya, peeled and cut in pieces

1 navel orange, peel removed and cut in sections

1 1/2 cups seedless grapes

1 banana, sliced

## DIRECTIONS

1. Mix all the cut up fruit.
2. Include the banana at the last second.

# Recipe 7 – Cucumber Salad

## Total Time: 5 Minutes

- **Preparation: 5 Mins**
- **Cooking: 0 Mins**

## *INGREDIENTS*

2 cucumbers, very thinly sliced

1 red onion, very thinly sliced

2 tbsps vinegar or 2 tbsps lemon juice

2 tbsps low-fat sour cream or 2 tbsps yogurt

salt and pepper, to taste (I like a lot of pepper)

1⁄2 tsp sugar

1 tsp chopped fresh dill

## <u>DIRECTIONS</u>

1. Blend cucumbers and onions with each other.
2. Blend rest of ingredients with each other in a shut pan and shake it.
3. Include to cucumbers, chill until very cold and serve.

# Recipe 8 - Mock Tuna Salad OR Chickpea Salad

## Total Time: 10 Minutes

- **Preparation: 10 Mins**
- **Cooking: 0 Mins**

## *INGREDIENTS*

1 (16 ounce) can chickpeas, mashed (garbanzo beans)

2 tbsps mayonnaise

2 tsps spicy brown mustard

1 tbsp sweet pickle relish

2 green onions, finely chopped

salt and pepper

1 tbsp finely minced yellow onion (optional)

## DIRECTIONS

1. In a medium pan
2. combine mayonnaise, mashed chickpeas, relish, mustard, sliced green onions, pepper, salt, and yellow onion (if preferred).
3. Blend properly.

# Recipe 9 - No Fat Carrot Raisin Salad

## Total Time: 10 Minutes

- **Preparation: 10 Mins**
- **Cooking: 0 Mins**

## *INGREDIENTS*

1⁄2 cup nonfat yogurt

1 1⁄2 tbsps honey

1 tbsp lemon juice

1⁄4 tsp cinnamon

2 cups carrots, shredded

1⁄2 cup raisins

1⁄4 cup crushed pineapple, drained

## DIRECTIONS

1. Mix honey, yogurt, cinnamon and juice of lemons to create dressing.
2. Include the rest of the ingredients.
3. Chill a minimum of 16 mins.

# Recipe 10 - Picnic Salad

## Total Time: 10 Minutes

- **Preparation: 10 Mins**
- **Cooking: 0 Mins**

## *INGREDIENTS*

4 cups cooked pasta, drained and rinsed in cold water (I like the multi-color variety for visual effect)

1 cup chopped green onion

2 cups diced tomatoes

1 (4 ounce) canchopped green chilies, drained

1 cup sweet corn (frozen or canned)

2 tbsps chopped fresh cilantro

2 tbsps lime juice

2/3 cup picante sauce or 2/3 cup salsa

mayonnaise

1/2 cup sliced black olives (optional)

## _DIRECTIONS_

1. In salad pan, mix onions, salsa, tomato, pasta, corn, chilies, cilantro, lime lime juice (or if you have to lemon juice) and olives.
2. Stir to mix.
3. Include adequate mayonnaise to coating ingredients.
4. Refrigerate a few hours prior to serving.

# Recipe 11 - Easy Chickpea Salad

## Total Time: 10 Minutes

- **Preparation: 10 Mins**
- **Cooking: 0 Mins**

## *INGREDIENTS*

1 (15 ounce) can chickpeas, rinsed and drained (or about 2 cups cooked)

1/3-1/2 cup vegan mayonnaise (such as Vegenaise)

1 1/2 stalks celery, diced (optional)

1/2 tsp onion powder or 1/4 cup onion, minced

1/8 tsp garlic powder (to taste)

salt (to taste)

pepper (to taste)

## DIRECTIONS

1. In a pan, mash chickpeas along with a potato masher or fork
2. Keep a few chunks in for texture.
3. Stir in leftover ingredients till properly mixed.
4. This maintains in the refrigerator for a number of days.

# Recipe 12 - Fresh Tomato and Corn Salad

## Total Time: 15 Minutes

- **Preparation: 15 Mins**
- **Cooking: 0 Mins**

## *INGREDIENTS*

2 large fresh tomatoes (I like creole and beefsteak) or 2 lbs cherry tomatoes

1 1/2 cups fresh corn or 1 1/2 cups frozen corn, blanched and drained

8 fresh basil leaves

balsamic vinegar

extra virgin olive oil

## _DIRECTIONS_

1. Clean tomatoes and get rid of leaves
2. slice in to bite sized parts or pieces Tear basil leaves in to tiny pieces Mix tomato, basil and corn in a pan Drizzle along with balsamic vinegar and great olive oil, to taste.
3. Stir.
4. Now let chill for An hour for flavor blend, or serve right away for freshest display.
5. Stir prior to serving.

# Recipe 13 - Fruit Salad With Pudding

## Total Time: 10 Minutes

- **Preparation: 10 Mins**
- **Cooking: 0 Mins**

## *INGREDIENTS*

1 (29 ounce) can peach slices, undrained

1 (20 ounce) can pineapple chunks, undrained

1 (3 1/8 ounce) boxdry vanilla instant pudding mix

1 lb strawberry, stemmed and quartered

1 banana, sliced

1⁄2 pint blueberries

1 bunch grapes (I use the red ones)

1 -2 tbsp sugar (optional)

## DIRECTIONS

1. In a big bowl, mix pineapples, peaches, and vanilla pudding blend.
2. This consists of the juices from the cans.
3. Blend properly till pudding is dissolved.
4. Stir in banana, blueberries, strawberries, grapes, and sugar if preferred.
5. Chill.

# Recipe 14 - Kiwi Salad

## Total Time: 5 Minutes

- **Preparation: 5 Mins**
- **Cooking: 0 Mins**

## *INGREDIENTS*

6 kiwi, peeled and sliced

1 cup sliced strawberry

1 cup fresh pineapple, cut into 1 inch pieces

1 tbsp lemon juice

1 tsp honey

## DIRECTIONS

1. Blend all ingredients with each other and serve right away.

# Recipe 15 - Carrot and Raisin Salad With Pineapple

## Total Time: 10 Minutes

- **Preparation: 10 Mins**
- **Cooking: 0 Mins**

## *INGREDIENTS*

2/3 cup raisins

2 cups coarsely grated carrots

1 cup crushed pineapple, drained

1/3 cup mayonnaise-type salad dressing

1 tbsp lemon juice

1/4 tsp salt

1 tbsp sugar

## DIRECTIONS

1. Toss carrots, raisins and pineapple with each other softly; set aside.
2. Stir with each other mayo salt, juice of lemons, and sugar as well as include to the raisin blend.
3. Refrigerate till served.

# Recipe 16 - Insanely Easy Tomato Salad

## Total Time: 10 Minutes

- **Preparation: 10 Mins**
- **Cooking: 0 Mins**

## *INGREDIENTS*

4 medium tomatoes, cubed

1 garlic clove, crushed

2 tbsps chopped fresh basil (or to taste)

1 medium red onion, sliced thin

1⁄4 cup Italian dressing

## DIRECTIONS

1. Blend all ingredients and refrigerate.

# Time To Make 15-30 Minutes

## Recipe 17 - German Potato Salad

### Total Time: 30 Minutes

- **Preparation: 10 Mins**
- **Cooking: 20 Mins**

## *INGREDIENTS*

10 slices bacon, diced

1 cup sugar (or less)

1 cup distilled white vinegar

2 eggs

1 tsp salt

1 tsp prepared mustard

1 dash cayenne pepper

10 large potatoes, boiled

1 medium onion, sliced (optional)

## DIRECTIONS

1. Chop and fry bacon.
2. In a tiny pan, include salt, eggs, mustard, vinegar, sugar and cayenne pepper.
3. Beat properly and put into hot skillet along with bacon grease and bacon stirring right up until thickened.
4. Include diced cooked potatoes as well as chopped up onion.
5. Serve hot.

# Recipe 18 - Winter Fruit Salad

## Total Time: 30 Minutes

- **Preparation: 20 Mins**
- **Cooking: 10 Mins**

## *INGREDIENTS*

1 (20 ounce) can pineapple chunks

1⁄2 cup sugar

2 tbsps cornstarch

1⁄3 cup orange juice

1 tbsp lemon juice

1 (11 ounce) can mandarin oranges (drained)

3 -4 unpeeled apples, chopped (use green and red)

2 -3 bananas (sliced)

## DIRECTIONS

1. Drain pineapple, saving 3/4 cup juice.
2. Within a saucepan, mix cornstarch and sugar.
3. Include orange juice, pineapple juice and juice of lemons.
4. Cook and stir above medium heat till thickened and bubbly
5. cook and stir 2 minute more.
6. Take out from the heat; set aside.
7. In a pan, mix oranges, apples, pineapple chunks and bananas.
8. Put hot sauce on the fruit; stir lightly to coat.
9. Cover and put in fridge.

# Recipe 19 - Frog Eye Salad

## Total Time: 26 Minutes

- **Preparation: 15 Mins**
- **Cooking: 11 Mins**

## *INGREDIENTS*

1 1⁄3 cups acini di pepe pasta (uncooked)

1 (20 ounce) can pineapple chunks, drained (reserving 1/4 cup juice)

1 3⁄4 cups milk

1⁄4 cup sugar

1 (3 1/2 ounce) package instant vanilla pudding (I use regular, not sugar-free) or 1 (1 1/2 ounce) boxsugar free vanilla pudding (I use regular, not sugar-free)

1 (8 ounce) can crushed pineapple, drained

2 (12 ounce) cans mandarin orange sections, drained

3 cups mini marshmallows

1⁄2 cup flaked coconut

## DIRECTIONS

1. Cook pasta in boiling water for 12 minutes.
2. Drain properly, rinsing out using cold water to cool pasta.
3. Inside big pan, beat reserved milk, sugar, pineapple juice, and pudding blend for 3 minutes.
4. Carefully stir in pasta and other ingredients.
5. Cover and refrigerate a minimum of 6 hours.

# Recipe 20 - Kamaboko Salad

## Total Time: 20 Minutes

- **Preparation: 10 Mins**
- **Cooking: 10 Mins**

## *INGREDIENTS*

8 ounces imitation crab sticks (kamaboko)

1 cup celery, chopped (or shredded cabbage)

4 ounces pasta (small shells or any other, cooked and seasoned with salt)

1 tbsp green onion, chopped

1/4 cup mayonnaise (or to taste)

salt and pepper (to taste)

## DIRECTIONS

1. Slice the crab sticks or kamaboko in to slim pieces horizontally.
2. Blend all the ingredients with each other.
3. Serve on lettuce leaves.

# Recipe 21 - Watermelon Salad with Feta

## Total Time: 20 Minutes

- **Preparation: 20 Mins**
- **Cooking: 0 Mins**

## *INGREDIENTS*

1⁄4 cup extra virgin olive oil

1 1⁄2 tbsps fresh lemon juice

1⁄2 tsp harissa or 1⁄2 tsp hot sauce

salt

fresh ground pepper

1 1⁄2 lbs seedless watermelon, rind removed,fruit sliced 1/4 inch thick

1⁄2 small red onion, thinly sliced

1⁄4 cup coarsely chopped flat leaf parsley

1⁄4 cup pitted oil-cured black olive, coarsely chopped

2 ounces feta cheese, crumbled (about 1/2 c.)

## DIRECTIONS

1. Within a tiny pan, whisk the olive oil along with the harissa and juice of lemons and season using pepper and salt.
2. Set up the watermelon pieces on a platter and spread along with parsley, olives, the onion and feta.
3. Drizzle the dressing on top and eat.

# Recipe 22 - Tuna-Noodle Salad

## Total Time: 30 Minutes

- **Preparation: 15 Mins**
- **Cooking: 15 Mins**

## *INGREDIENTS*

1 (12 ounce) package egg noodles, cooked

2 (12 1/2 ounce) cans tuna in water

1 cup green onion, chopped

3 hard-boiled eggs, chopped

4 tbsps mayonnaise (add more if desired)

1 tsp season salt

1 tsp ground pepper

2 tbsps dill relish or 2 tbsps chopped dill pickles

1 cup celery, chopped

## <u>DIRECTIONS</u>

1. Boil water in a 5 quart skillet and cook egg noodles to al dente.
2. Drain and allow it to cool.
3. Drain Tuna and mix with onion, celery mayo, and dill pickle relish include sliced boiled eggs. Blend properly.
4. Include ground pepper and season salt and blend properly.
5. Taste. Include much more seasoning or mayo to your preference.
6. Most effective if chilled for a minimum of An hour.
7. Serve cold.

# Recipe 23 – Low-Fat Black Bean And Corn Salad

## Total Time: 20 Minutes

- **Preparation: 20 Mins**
- **Cooking: 0 Mins**

## *INGREDIENTS*

2 cups canned black beans, drained and rinsed

2 cups crisp canned corn, drained

1/3 cup chopped red onion

1/4 cup chopped fresh cilantro

3 tbsps lime juice

1 tsp olive oil

1/2 tsp salt

1/2 tsp ground cumin

1/8 tsp ground red pepper

## DIRECTIONS

1. Blend all ingredients and chill immediately.
2. Spoon out A HALF servings as required.

# Recipe 24 - Watermelon and Cucumber Salad

## Total Time: 25 Minutes

- **Preparation: 10 Mins**
- **Cooking: 15 Mins**

## *INGREDIENTS*

3 cups seedless watermelon, chunked

2 cucumbers, sliced

1 jalapeno pepper

2 tbsps red wine vinegar

1/4 tsp salt

# DIRECTIONS

1. Seed and cut the jalapeno pepper.
2. Blend cucumbers, the watermelon and jalapeno with each other.
3. Include salt and vinegar and blend properly.
4. Let stand a minimum of 16 mins for the flavors in order to mix.

# Recipe 25 - Snap Pea Salad

## Total Time: 20 Minutes

- **Preparation: 10 Mins**
- **Cooking: 10 Mins**

## *INGREDIENTS*

1 lb snap peas, trimmed and cut into 1/4 inch pieces

1 cup red onion, finely chopped

1 small garlic clove, finely minced (optional)

3 tbsps lemon juice, fresh

2 tbsps oil, your favorite

salt and pepper, to taste

## <u>DIRECTIONS</u>

1. Mix all ingredients in a pan.
2. Let stand 5 to 10 minutes, tossing from time to time.

# Recipe 26 - BLT Macaroni Salad

## Total Time: 30 Minutes

- **Preparation: 15 Mins**
- **Cooking: 15 Mins**

## *INGREDIENTS*

1/2 cup mayonnaise

3 tbsps chili sauce

2 tbsps lemon juice

1 tsp sugar

3 cups elbow macaroni, cooked

1/2 cup tomatoes, seeded and chopped

2 tbsps green onions, chopped

3 cups lettuce, shredded

4 slices cooked bacon, crumbled

## DIRECTIONS

1. In a big pan, mix the first 4 ingredients; blend properly.
2. Include tomato, the macaroni and onions; toss to coat.
3. Cover and refrigerate.
4. Prior to serving, put bacon and lettuce; toss to coat.

# Recipe 27 - Quinoa Corn Salad

## Total Time: 30 Minutes

- **Preparation: 30 Mins**
- **Cooking: 0 Mins**

## *INGREDIENTS*

3 cups water

1 tsp salt

1 1⁄2 cups quinoa, thoroughly rinsed

2 cups fresh corn (frozen is okay)

1 cup fresh basil, tightly packed, finely chopped

1⁄2 cup diced roasted red pepper

1⁄2 cup finely diced red onion

2 tbsps olive oil

3 -5 tbsps fresh lemon juice

## DIRECTIONS

1. Bring water to a boil. Include quinoa and cook for around 12 minutes.
2. Include corn and simmer yet another 2 to 4 minutes.
3. Move quinoa and corn to a pan.
4. Stir to fluff and put aside to cool.
5. Stir in red peppers, basil, onions, and olive oil.
6. Include salt if required. Stir in juice of lemons to taste.

# Recipe 28 - Curried Couscous Salad

## Total Time: 25 Minutes

- **Preparation: 15 Mins**
- **Cooking: 10 Mins**

## *INGREDIENTS*

1 cup uncooked couscous

1 1⁄4 cups boiling water

1 medium tomatoes, chopped

1 green bell pepper, chopped

1 (15 ounce) can chickpeas, drained and rinsed

1 (8 ounce) container plain yogurt (or soy yogurt to make this dairy-free)

1 -1 1⁄2 tsp curry powder

salt and pepper

## DIRECTIONS

1. Put couscous in a big pan and pour boiling water over the top.
2. Allow it to soak for 5 to 10 minutes in order to swell the grains, after that fluff it using a fork.
3. Include the leftover ingredients to the couscous and also stir properly to blend.
4. Chill in the refrigerator and serve.

# Recipe 29 - Chickpea, Couscous and Cranberry Salad

## Total Time: 20 Minutes

- **Preparation: 10 Mins**
- **Cooking: 10 Mins**

## *INGREDIENTS*

1 cup chicken stock

1 cup couscous

1⁄2 tsp curry powder (optional)

3⁄4 cup canned chick-peas, rinsed and drained

1⁄3 cup dried cranberries

1⁄4 cup green onion, chopped

1⁄4 cup red bell pepper, diced

1⁄4 cup fresh basil, chopped

## DIRECTIONS

1. Bring stock to a boil in tiny saucepan as well as stir in couscous and curry powder, cover and let stand for around 6 minutes. Move mixture to a big pan to let cool.
2. Stir cranberries, green onions, chickpeas, bell pepper, and basil directly into the couscous.
3. For the dressing, blend with each other orange juice, the olive oil, orange rind, honey and garlic.
4. Put on couscous and serve.

# Recipe 30 - Soba Salad With Miso Dressing

## Total Time: 20 Minutes

- **Preparation: 15 Mins**
- **Cooking: 5 Mins**

## *INGREDIENTS*

3 -4 ounces soba noodles

1 carrot, peeled and finely chopped

2 cups edamame (frozen are fine)

3 -4 tbsps soy sauce

1 lime, juice of

2 tbsps miso (white or light)

1 tbsp mirin or 1 tsp sugar, to taste

1 (10 ounce) package spinach, fresh washed and trimmed

1/4 cup scallion, chopped

salt and pepper, to taste

1 tbsp ginger, freshly grated

## DIRECTIONS

1. Bring a large pot of water to a boil and salt it.
2. Drop in the noodles and carrot and cook until tender, 2 to 4 minutes
3. Add the edamame for about 30 seconds to 1 minute just to warm, then drain everything in a colander.
4. Put aside.
5. In a big salad pan, whisk with each other the soy sauce, lime juice, mirin or sugar and miso.
6. Include noodles, spinach, edamame, carrot, scallion and toss
7. after that taste and season using salt and pepper as necessary. Garnish using grated ginger at the kitchen table.

# Recipe 31 - Couscous Pepper Salad

## Total Time: 30 Minutes

- **Preparation: 15 Mins**
- **Cooking: 15 Mins**

## *INGREDIENTS*

2 cups water (or vegetable broth)

1 cup israeli couscous

1 tsp olive oil

1⁄2 tsp kosher salt

1 1⁄2 cups kidney beans, rinsed and drained (or black beans)

3⁄4 cup chopped red bell pepper

3⁄4 cup chopped green bell pepper

1⁄4 cup chopped red onion

3 green onions, chopped

1⁄2 cup chopped fresh cilantro

1⁄4 cup chopped fresh flat leaf parsley

1⁄4-1⁄2 tsp red pepper flakes (optional)

1 tbsp honey

1 large lime, juice of

3 tbsps extra virgin olive oil

salt and pepper

# *DIRECTIONS*

1. Bring water to a boil.
2. Include olive oil, couscous, and salt. cook for around 12 to 15 minutes or till tender to the bite.
3. Drain and cool couscous.
4. Mix couscous along with peppers, kidney beans, green onion, onion, cilantro, parsley and hot pepper flakes.
5. Whisk with each other lime juice, honey, olive oil and mix with couscous blend.
6. Season using extra salt and pepper. Enjoy!

# Recipe 32 - Macaroni Ham Salad

## Total Time: 25 Minutes

- **Preparation: 25 Mins**
- **Cooking: 0 Mins**

## *INGREDIENTS*

2 cups macaroni, cooked

1 cup canned ham, chopped (or a small can of Hormel type shredded)

1⁄2 cup celery, chopped

1⁄4 cup onion, finely chopped

1⁄4 cup sweet pickle relish

1⁄2 cup muenster cheese, cubed

mayonnaise

# *DIRECTIONS*

1. In a big pan, mix all ingredients other than the mayonnaise.
2. Right after combining everything, include sufficient mayonnaise to suit your tastes.
3. Chill a minimum of A couple of hours prior to serving.

# Recipe 33 - Chicken Taco Salad

## Total Time: 17 Minutes

- **Preparation: 15 Mins**
- **Cooking: 2 Mins**

## *INGREDIENTS*

2 boneless skinless chicken breasts

1/2 tsp garlic salt

1 tbsp chili powder

lettuce, torn into bite-size pieces

1 cucumber, peeled and diced

1 cup shredded low-fat cheddar cheese

1 cup chunky salsa

1 tomatoes, chopped

3 green onions, chopped

fat free ranch dressing

baked corn tortilla chips

## _DIRECTIONS_

1. Sprinkle chicken using chili powder and garlic salt.
2. Broil A couple of minutes or till done.
3. Cool and slice into pieces.
4. In a pan, toss lettuce along with cucumber, chicken, and cheese.
5. To serve, top with tomato, green onions, salsa, dressing and smashed tortilla chips.

# Recipe 34 - Romaine Strawberry Salad

## Total Time: 20 Minutes

- **Preparation: 20 Mins**
- **Cooking: 0 Mins**

## *INGREDIENTS*

2 heads romaine lettuce

15 strawberries, sliced

1 small purple onion, sliced thin


**Dressing**

3⁄4 cup Hellmann's mayonnaise

1⁄2 cup sugar

1⁄4 cup milk

2 tbsps white vinegar

2 tbsps poppy seeds

## _DIRECTIONS_

1. Mix the ingredients for the dressing and toss
   with onions, lettuce, strawberry's and serve.

# Recipe 35 – Mccarron's Strawberry Feta Salad

## Total Time: 20 Minutes

- **Preparation: 20 Mins**
- **Cooking: 0 Mins**

## *INGREDIENTS*

1 head romaine lettuce

1⁄2 lb baby spinach leaves, fresh

1⁄2 cup walnuts, chopped

1 cup strawberry, sliced

1⁄4 cup feta cheese, crumbled

## _DIRECTIONS_

1. Don't preheat your stove.
2. Clean lettuce and spinach leaves.
3. Spin dry.
4. Place directly into salad pan along with next 2 ingredients.
5. Toss using balsamic vinaigrette.
6. Sprinkle feta cheese on top.

## Recipe 36 - Orange Creamsicle Salad

### Total Time: 35 Minutes

- **Preparation: 10 Mins**
- **Cooking: 25 Mins**

### *INGREDIENTS*

1 (3 1/4 ounce) package tapioca pudding

1 (3 1/2 ounce) package instant vanilla pudding

1 (3 ounce) package orange Jell-O

2 1⁄4 cups water

1 (8 ounce) container Cool Whip

2 (10 ounce) cans mandarin oranges, drained

# _DIRECTIONS_

1. Mix Jello, pudding mixes and water, stirring properly.
2. Cook above medium heat whilst stirring continuously till blend comes to a boil.
3. Cool to room heat.
4. Stir in Cool Whip and oranges.
5. Chill properly.
6. PLEASE NOTE: Despite the fact that this recipe is cooked, the vanilla pudding blend is immediate.
7. It isn't a mistake.

# Recipe 37 - Tuna and Brown Rice Salad

## Total Time: 35 Minutes

- **Preparation: 20 Mins**
- **Cooking: 15 Mins**

## *INGREDIENTS*

1 tbsp sweet pickle relish

1 tbsp red wine vinegar

2 tsps canola oil

1⁄2 tsp spicy mustard or 1⁄2 tsp Dijon mustard

1 cup cooked brown rice

3 ounces drained tuna fish

1⁄4 cup shredded carrot

1⁄4 cup diced cucumber

# <u>DIRECTIONS</u>

1. Blend vinegar, oil, relish and mustard.
2. Include leftover ingredients as well as toss in order to coat.
3. Let to marinate in the fridge a minimum of 15 mins prior to serving.

# Recipe 38 - Potato and Beet Salad

## Total Time: 45 Minutes

- **Preparation: 20 Mins**
- **Cooking: 25 Mins**

## *INGREDIENTS*

1⁄3 cup white vinegar (or use the juice from the pickled beets for more vibrant color)

1 tsp salt

1⁄2-1 tsp pepper

1⁄2 tsp fresh horseradish

2 tbsps fresh parsley

1 cup mayonnaise (adding more after tossing with salad ingredients for more creaminess if desired)

## DIRECTIONS

1. Blend all of salad dressing ingredients in a big pan.

2. Toss leftover ingredients in to the big pan along with dressing, toss to coat.

3. Chill for a minimum of An hour over night is most effective.

4. Top with chopped up egg and spread paprika.

# Recipe 39 - Lentil and Yogurt Salad

## Total Time: 35 Minutes

- **Preparation: 5 Mins**
- **Cooking: 30 Mins**

## *INGREDIENTS*

1 cup dry lentils, rinsed (I used green)

6 cups water

2 cups nonfat yogurt (original has 6 cups!)

1⁄4 cup fresh cilantro, chopped

2 garlic cloves, minced

1 tsp dried thyme

1 pinch cayenne

salt and pepper, to taste

# DIRECTIONS

1. Put lentils and water in a sauce pot and bring to a boil.
2. Cover and cook above medium heat for 27-30 minutes or till lentils are tender yet not mushy.
3. Drain and permit to cool.
4. Put cooled lentils in a blending pan and stir in the remaining of the ingredients.
5. Recommended to serve instantly.

# Recipe 40 - Blueberry Couscous Salad

## Total Time: 40 Minutes

- **Preparation: 30 Mins**
- **Cooking: 10 Mins**

## *INGREDIENTS*

1⁄2 cup orange juice

1⁄3 cup water

1⁄2 tsp salt, divided

3⁄4 cup wholewheat couscous

1 cup blueberries

1 cup mango, cut into cubes

1⁄3 cup red onion, chopped

2 tbsps mint, chopped

2 tbsps lemon juice

2 tbsps olive oil

1⁄8 tsp pepper

# DIRECTIONS

1. Mix oj and water and QUARTER tsp salt in saucepan, bring to boil above medium heat and after that stir in the couscous; cover

2. take away from heat and let stand A few minutes.

3. Move to pan and fluff using a fork; cool 5 to 10 minutes.

4. Stir in leftover QUARTER tsp salt and the remaining of the ingredients.

5. Toss to blend properly.

# Recipe 41 - Mediterranean-Style Orzo Salad With Corn

## Total Time: 60 Minutes

- **Preparation: 50 Mins**
- **Cooking: 10 Mins**

## *INGREDIENTS*

1 lb orzo pasta

2 cups fresh corn kernels, cut off the cob

1 cup finely chopped red sweet bell pepper

1 cup kalamata olive, pitted, cut in half

1/4 cup thinly sliced scallion (white and green parts)

2 tbsps coarsely chopped basil (regular or opal)

2 tbsps drained capers

1/4 cup packed fresh parsley leaves, finely chopped

1/4 cup olive oil

3 tbsps wine vinegar (we used red wine vinegar)

1⁄8 tsp salt (to taste)

fresh ground black pepper, to taste

fresh edible flower, such as fresh nasturtium (optional)

## DIRECTIONS

1. Bring a big pan of softly salted water to a boil.
2. Include the orzo and simmer, stirring from time to time, for around 10 minutes, or till tender.
3. Drain properly and move to a big serving pan.
4. Include red pepper, olives, the corn as well as scallions and toss properly.
5. Include capers, vinegar, the basil, oil, parsley, salt and pepper and softly toss.
6. Enhance the salad using the edible flowers prior to serving.

# Recipe 42 – Green-Onion and Potato Salad

## Total Time: 40 Minutes

- **Preparation: 10 Mins**
- **Cooking: 30 Mins**

## *INGREDIENTS*

6 large potatoes, scrubbed

1/3 cup oil

1/4 cup red wine vinegar

1/4 cup water

1/4 cup chopped green onion

1 pimiento, minced (optional)

1 garlic clove, minced (optional)

1/4 tsp ground black pepper

salt, to taste

## <u>DIRECTIONS</u>

1.  Boil the potatoes in their jackets. When finished, the moment you can handle them, peel off and cut around A QUARTER inch to A HALF inch thick.
2.  Whilst the potatoes are cooking, blend with each other the rest of the ingredients.
3.  Put the chopped up potatoes in a pan.
4.  Stir with each other the dressing and put on the hot potatoes.
5.  Using a big spoon, toss the salad cautiously to coat.
6.  warm it up in the microwave.

# Recipe 43 - Hot German Potato Salad

## Total Time: 45 Minutes

- **Preparation: 30 Mins**
- **Cooking: 15 Mins**

## *INGREDIENTS*

4 potatoes, sliced in chunks

1 small onion, sliced in rings

1 -1 1⁄2 cup Italian salad dressing

## DIRECTIONS

1. Boil your potatoes in hot salted water.
2. Drain and instantly include the onion.
3. After that include your salad dressing.
4. Toss till coated.
5. Eat warm and enjoy.

# Recipe 44 - Turkish Bulgur Wheat Salad

## Total Time: 50 Minutes

- **Preparation: 25 Mins**
- **Cooking: 25 Mins**

## *INGREDIENTS*

1 medium cooking onion, chopped and sauteed

2 cups bulgur (add 4 cups of boiled water in a bowl and set aside)

3 freshly squeezed lemons

1/2 cup finely chopped parsley

1 large tomatoes, diced

1/4 tsp cumin

1/4 tsp coriander

1/4 tsp paprika

1 cup quartered red seedless grapes or 1 cup quartered green seedless grape

1/4 cup extra virgin olive oil

salt

## *DIRECTIONS*

1. Blend all the ingredients with each other and allow it to marinate for a minimum of a 1 / 2 hour in the fridge after that serve.
2. Whenever pomegranates are in season.
3. replace the grape, helps make for attractive color.

# Recipe 45 - Baked Potato Salad

## <u>Total Time: 55 Minutes</u>

- **Preparation: 10 Mins**
- **Cooking: 45 Mins**

## *<u>INGREDIENTS</u>*

7 medium red potatoes, about 3 pounds

2 cups light cheddar cheese

8 ounces fat free ranch dressing

1 tbsp prepared mustard

6 green onions, chopped

1 medium red bell pepper, chopped

2 slices bacon, cooked and crumbled

# DIRECTIONS

1. Coat potatoes along with veggie cooking spray; pierce many times using a fork.
2. Bake at 420 degree for 40 minutes or till tender.
3. Cool and slice in to 1 inch cubes.
4. Mix 1 and a HALF cups cheese, dressing as well as following 3 ingredients in a big pan.
5. Include potatoes, tossing softly.
6. Sprinkle using bacon and leftover a HALF cup cheese.

# Recipe 46 - Beet Salad with yogurt

## Total Time: 40 Minutes

- **Preparation: 10 Mins**
- **Cooking: 30 Mins**

## *INGREDIENTS*

4 medium peeled beets, , cooked,cooled and cut into small dice

16 ounces plain low-fat yogurt

chopped fresh dill (, for garnish)

# <u>DIRECTIONS</u>

1. Fold the beets softly in to the yogurt.
2. Put in a serving pan and garnish using sliced dill.

# Recipe 47 - Chicken Pasta Salad

## Total Time: 40 Minutes

- **Preparation: 20 Mins**
- **Cooking: 20 Mins**

## *INGREDIENTS*

3 1/2 cups small seashell macaroni, cooked without salt and oil

3 cups small fresh broccoli florets

1 3/4 cups trimmed fresh snow peas

1 2/3 cups chopped cooked chicken

1 cup red bell pepper, strips

1/4 cup sliced green onion

5 tbsps red wine vinegar

3 tbsps vegetable oil

2 tbsps honey

2 tsps sesame seeds, toasted

1 tsp hot sauce

1/2 tsp salt

1/2 tsp ground ginger

3 garlic cloves, minced

## DIRECTIONS

1. Mix first 6 ingredients in a big pan; toss well.
2. Mix vinegar and next 7 ingredients in a tiny pan; stir properly.
3. Put dressing on pasta blend; toss soft.
4. Cover and chill a minimum of A couple of hours.

# Recipe 48 - Red Cabbage Salad With Raisins, Apples and Honey Dressing

## Total Time: 37 Minutes

- **Preparation: 20 Mins**
- **Cooking: 17 Mins**

## *INGREDIENTS*

1 medium head red cabbage, shredded

3⁄4 cup apple juice

salt (to taste)

2 apples, peeled, cored and diced

1⁄2 cup golden raisin

4 tbsps cider vinegar

4 tbsps honey

1 tbsp oil

## DIRECTIONS

1. In a Dutch stove, put apple juice, cabbage, and salt.
2. Cook blend for 15 mins.
3. Include raisins and the apples and carry on cooking till apples and cabbage are tender and the majority of the liquid is soaked up.
4. Stir together honey, the vinegar, and oil till mixed.
5. Put dressing on the cabbage and cook blend for A couple of minutes or till heated through.
6. Refrigerate till serving time, and eat.

# Recipe 49 - Raspberry Tapioca Salad

## Total Time: 35 Minutes

- **Preparation: 15 Mins**
- **Cooking: 20 Mins**

## *INGREDIENTS*

4 cups water

1⁄2 cup sugar

1⁄2 cup pearl tapioca

1 (3 ounce) package raspberry Jell-O gelatin

1 (8 ounce) Cool Whip

1 (10 ounce) bag frozen raspberries

## DIRECTIONS

1. Bring sugar, water, and tapioca to a boil, stirring frequently till the tapioca is clear.
2. Take away from heat and also put the package of jello.
3. Cool to set till regularity is like jelly.
4. Include cool whip and freezing raspberries.
5. Stir properly and refrigerate.

# Recipe 50 - Jalapeno Potato Salad

## Total Time: 40 Minutes

- **Preparation: 10 Mins**
- **Cooking: 30 Mins**

## *INGREDIENTS*

2 lbs baby red potatoes

3 -4 tbsps mayonnaise

1 jalapeno pepper, finely chopped (I add more for extra heat!)

2 green onions (increase if you increase mayo)

1 tbsp fresh cilantro, finely chopped (increase if you increase mayo)

salt and pepper

## DIRECTIONS

1.  Simmer non-peeled red potatoes for 18-20 minutes.
2.  Cool, Cube potatoes.
3.  mix all ingredients in big pan.
4.  Season using pepper and salt to taste.

# The End and More

**We reached the end of the book, I hope you enjoyed it.**

**Here are some authors, sources and books that helped me to write this book:**

20 Healthy Copycat Restaurant Recipes: Healthy Homemade Copycat Recipes From Famous Restaurants, Bring Your Favorite Restaurant To Your Home Kindle Edition

by Maira Benjamin

Food.com

Slow Cooker Recipes: 30 Of The Most Healthy And Delicious Slow Cooker Recipes: Includes New Recipes For 2015 With Fantastic Ingredients Kindle Edition

by Stacey Turner

allrecipes.com

The Clean Eating Cookbook & Diet: Over 100 Healthy Whole Food Recipes & Meal Plans

recipe.com

The Skinnytaste Cookbook: Light on Calories, Big on Flavor Kindle Edition

by Gina Homolka

Clean Food Diet: Avoid processed foods and eat clean with few simple lifestyle changes(free nutrition recipes)(natural food recipes) (Special Diet Cookbooks & Vegetarian Recipes Collection Book 4) Kindle Edition

by Jonathan Vine

# Conclusion

Thank you again for downloading the book.

Finally. I hope you enjoyed this book. **Please take the time to share your thoughts and post a review on Amazon. It'd be greatly appreciated.**

Thank you and good luck !

Anita.

Printed in Great
Britain
by Amazon